Usborne
Little First Colouring
Things that go

Illustrated by Jenny Brown

Words by Kirsteen Robson

A plane flies high.

A car goes on roads.

A steam engine
puffs.

A rocket
zooms.

A boat sails on water.

A bus is big.

A bin lorry collects rubbish.

A digger
scoops earth.

A motorbike
is noisy.

A helicopter hovers.

A truck carries things.

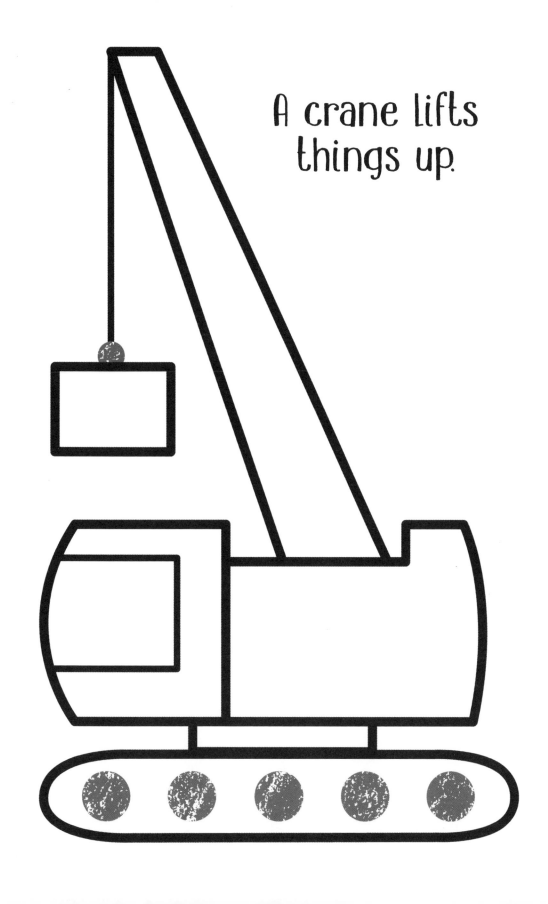

A crane lifts things up.

Racing cars
go very fast.

A ferry chugs
slowly.

A van hurries along.

A roller-coaster
rides on rails.

A balloon
drifts.

A submarine
dives deep.

A tractor in mud

A seaplane
landing

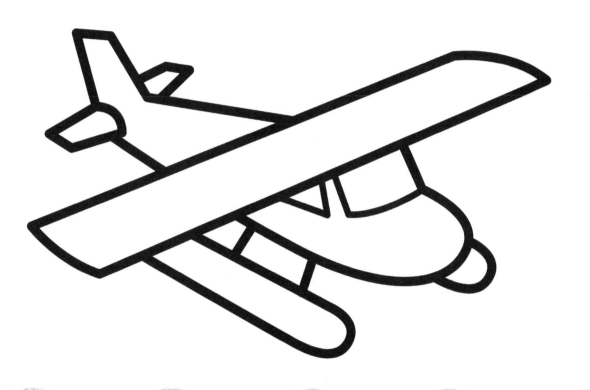

A fire engine wails.

A forklift beeps.

A go-kart whizzes
around a track.

A tram joins to electric wires.

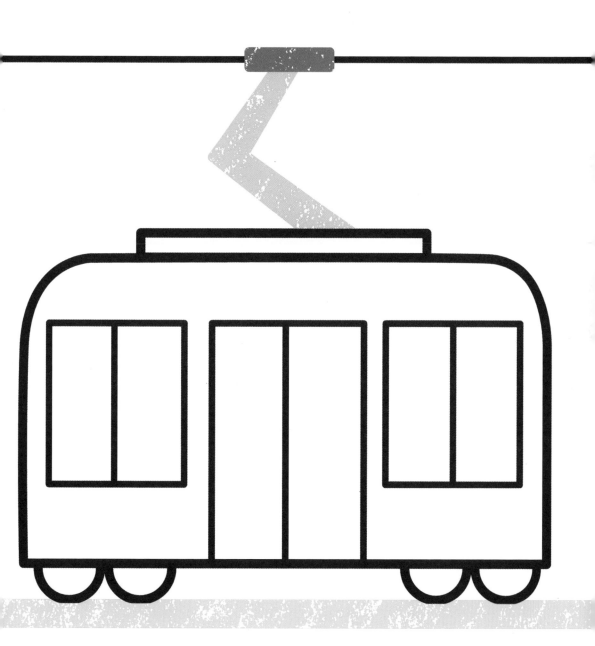

A cable car
up high

A motorhome
on grass

A recovery truck and
broken-down car

A fishing boat at sea

Trains go through tunnels.

A dump truck
carries earth.

A parachute
floats down.